HATE SP...
regulation
Commercial Speech
First Amendment
fair trial   free press
LIBEL   Invasion
             privacy
CENSORSHIP FREEDOM OF SPEECH trademark confidentiality
Freedom
of the Press
COPYRIGHT

COMMUNICATION LAW

Eddith A. Dashiell, Ph.D.

Kendall Hunt
publishing company

Cover image © Shutterstock, Inc.

Kendall Hunt
publishing company

www.kendallhunt.com
Send all inquiries to:
4050 Westmark Drive
Dubuque, IA 52004-1840

Copyright © 2014 by Kendall Hunt Publishing Company

ISBN 978-1-5249-1281-9

Printed in the United States of America

Contents

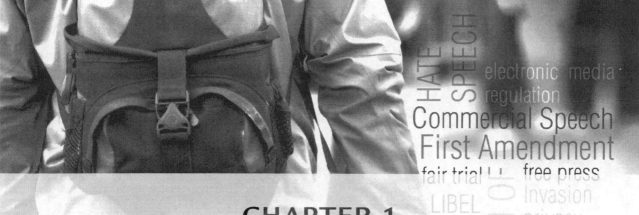

CHAPTER 1

COURSE OVERVIEW AND OBJECTIVES

> ### Jour 3100/5100   Communication Law (3 cr. hrs)
>
> INSTRUCTOR: Dr. Eddith A. Dashiell (Dr. D.)
>
> OFFICE: Schoonover Center 232 **E-MAIL:** dashiell@ohio.edu
>
> PHONE: 740.593.2550 **FAX:** 740.593.2592
>
> OFFICE HOURS : Posted on your **J3100/5100 Blackboard** site
>
> SYLLABUS, ASSIGNMENTS & DEADLINES : Posted on your **J3100/5100 Blackboard** site

Course Objectives

It is not my goal to inspire all of you to become attorneys. Instead, the purpose of this course is to make you conversant with laws and legal concepts that affect the mass media and able to discuss, apply and write about them intelligently, conversationally and jargon free.

By the end of this semester you should be able to:

- **Demonstrate** a good understanding of how the courts have balanced the First Amendment right of freedom of speech and of the press with other important governmental interests (i.e., national security, civil rights, privacy, libel, advertising, indecent language, copyright, access to information, confidentiality, free press v. fair trial, intellectual property, obscenity)

- **Demonstrate** a good understanding of how the First Amendment right of freedom of speech and of the press relate to you as a **citizen** as well as a communication professional

- **Demonstrate** an ability to analyze various viewpoints about how, why and when the First Amendment rights of the media should or should not be limited

- **Demonstrate** an understanding of gender, race, ethnicity, sexual orientation and other forms of diversity in U.S. society in relation to the First Amendment right of freedom of speech and of the press

- **Demonstrate** an ability to apply relevant case, administrative or statutory law to evaluate current issues involving the First Amendment protection of speech and press

- **Demonstrate** an ability to find **primary** legal sources (case law, statutory law, administrative law) using *Lexis-Nexis Academic*

- **Demonstrate** an ability to read, understand and explain the complicated legal jargon of a court decision

Core Requirement

This course is one of the core requirements for undergraduate majors in the E.W. Scripps School of Journalism. To remain active in the BSJ program, undergraduates must earn at least a C in all core courses. Graduate students must earn at least a B in order to remain active in the journalism graduate program.

Required Textbooks

- Refer to current term's syllabus posted on your J3100/5100 Blackboard site for assigned textbook(s).

Required Internet Resources

- *Lexis-Nexis Academic* via **Ohio University Libraries home page:** http://www.library.ohiou.edu/
- *Blackboard*, Ohio University's online course delivery and management system: https://blackboard.ohio.edu/ (Accessible via your "My OHIO" portal)
- **Ohio University email account**

Required Readings/Handouts (as assigned)

Located in the appropriate First Amendment topic folder located under your **JOUR 3100/5100** *Blackboard* **"Contents"** link

---

Class Expectations & Etiquette

- Bring your **required** supplement workbook (**Dashiell, Eddith.** *Communication Law*. **Kendall Hunt Publishing**) to every class session. You will find it extremely helpful in your note taking.
- **DO NOT TEXT DURING MY LECTURES!** It's rude and unprofessional! With the exception of laptop computers/tablets used **only** for note taking purposes, all electronic devices (i.e., cell phones, hand-held computer games, etc.) must be turned off. **No** electronic devices—**including** laptops/tablets—will be permitted during an in-class, timed exam.
- Check your **J3100/5100 Blackboard** link and your **Ohio University** email account daily for any class updates or revisions.

Attendance

Perfect attendance is expected. Attendance will be taken during every class session. Those who have **perfect** attendance may add 3 percentage points to their final grade. Those with no more than **two** absences may add 2 percentage points. Students with more than two absences are not eligible for any bonus points for attendance. **Excused** absences will allow you to make up any missed quizzes/exams or receive an extension of a paper deadline. However, excused absences (even university-sanctioned absences) will **NOT** count toward the 3-percentage-point bonus for **perfect** attendance. If you need to make up an exam or turn in an assignment late, the **only excused** absence is an absence that has been approved by me **in advance**. Your absence is **not** excused **unless** you get confirmation from me. Just because you send me an e-mail message about your absence does **not** automatically make your absence excused. **No** make-up exams or assignment extensions will be given for **unexcused** absences. When makeup exams will be scheduled and how they will be formatted are at my discretion.

Special Note

In any large-size class there is always a certain mutual anonymity between students and instructor. I would like to break down that anonymity as much as possible. **Please feel free to come by my office to visit.** You may come by during my office hours or make an appointment.

Accessibility Services

If you suspect that you may need an accommodation based on the impact of a disability, you should contact me privately to discuss your specific needs and provide written documentation from the Office of Student Accessibility Services. If you are not yet registered as a student with a disability, you should contact the Office of Student Accessibility Services - 348 Baker University Center, 740.593.2620, or http://www.ohio.edu/disabilities/. In compliance with the Americans with Disabilities Act (ADA), all qualified students enrolled in this course are entitled to "reasonable accommodations."

Exams

- Three exams (50 pts each). <Exams will **not** be returned.>
- Format: Combination of matching, multiple choice, short answer and/or essay questions

- In addition to knowing the jargon terms and other relevant material from class lectures, required text and workbook, and required *Blackboard* readings/handouts, be prepared to thoroughly discuss the following elements for each assigned court case:

  1. **Description:** What triggered the dispute; Who (full names and titles of plaintiffs) sued whom (full names and titles of defendants) and why (with specific examples/details). What were the plaintiff/appellee/petitioner's arguments? What were defendant/appellant/respondent's arguments?

  2. **Resolution:** Which court made the final decision; What the final court decision was (i.e., Who won and <u>why</u>; specific reasons how the court reached its decision (the court's rationale)

  3. **Significance:** What effect this court decision has had on this particular First Amendment issue?

  4. **Application:** Be able to <u>apply</u> the court's rationale in this specific decision to hypothetical scenarios involving this same First Amendment issue

Legal Research Exercises

- Two exercises (10 pts each).
- Submit via **email attachment** to *dashiell@ohio.edu* by the established deadline.
- Assignment instructions are posted on **Blackboard (JOUR 3100** *Blackboard* →Content→ "**Legal Research Exercises**" folder (contains instructions for **Legal Research Exercise #1 and Legal Research Exercise #2**)

Analysis Paper

- One analysis paper (100 pts.)
- Submit via **email attachment** to *dashiell@ohio.edu* by the established deadline.
- Assignment instructions are posted in the "**Analysis Paper**" folder (**JOUR 3100/5100** *Blackboard* →**Content**→ "**Analysis Paper**" folder
- The "**Analysis Paper**" folder contains detailed assignment instructions along with supplemental handouts (**i.e.,** FAQs; detailed instructions on how to find relevant case law). Please refer to these supplemental handouts, because they will be very help (and time saving) in completing this assignment

GRADING: Final Grades will be Tabulated on a Scale of 270 Points.

	Analysis Paper	Legal Research Exercises 10 pts each	Exams 50-pts each	270 total pts. (minimum pts. for grade)
A	92–100	10	46–50	249
A-	90–91	9	45	243
B+	87–89	—	44	235
B	82–86	—	41–43	221
B-	79–81	8	39–40	213
C+	77–78	—	37–38	208
C	72–76	—	36	194
D	60–71	7	31–35	167
F	≤59	≤6	≤30	≤166

Deadlines

Assignments may be turned in early, but never late. The penalty for late work is a full letter grade per day (24-hour period); Saturdays and Sundays included.

Assignment Deadlines and List of Cases

- Due dates for your assignments and the list of cases in the order of how they will be discussed in class are posted in your **J3100/5100 Blackboard "Contents" Link.**
- **CAUTION:** Because the First Amendment issues related to the media are in a constant state of change, **ASSIGNMENT DEADLINES** and **LIST OF CASES** are subject to change as well.
- **Always** refer to your **J3100/5100 Blackboard "Contents"** link for **any revisions** to class deadlines and list of cases.

Academic Integrity

"Ohio University holds as its central purpose the intellectual and personal development of its students. Distinguished by its rich history, diverse campus, international community, and beautiful Appalachian setting, Ohio University is known as well for its outstanding faculty of accomplished teachers whose research and creative activity advance knowledge across many disciplines."(Ohio University Mission Statement, Reprinted with permission of Ohio University). Part of this process includes the expectation that students will be honest and forthright in their academic endeavors. Academic honesty is expected at **all** times. All forms of academic misconduct are a Code A violation of the Ohio University Code of Student Conduct. Examples of academic misconduct include (but are **not** limited to) copying from others or using notes, books or electronic technology during an exam (cheating), taking an exam or similar evaluation in the place of another person; permitting another student to cheat from you, acquiring or giving improper knowledge of an exam, signing in persons other than yourself for class attendance; allowing another class member to sign your name on the attendance sheet; submitting the same paper in two different courses without the knowledge and consent of both instructors, or turning in a paper or project that is not your work (plagiarism). Plagiarism also includes excessive "copying and pasting" from the Internet with no evidence of re-writing or personal analysis. If you are found to be involved in academic misconduct, you will receive an "F" grade on the project or for the class and a referral to the Director of Community Standards & Student Responsibility with the possible sanction of suspension or expulsion. You have the right to appeal academic sanctions through the grade appeal process. See:

Ohio University Office of Community Standards and Student Responsibility, *Student Code of Conduct Policies* at http://www.ohio.edu/communitystandards/code/index.cfm

Grade Appeal

You have the right to appeal any grade in any course. Talk with me informally about any concerns you may have about your grade. If you are not satisfied, you may use the Scripps College of Communication's three-level appeal procedure: Level 1: You are required to submit your appeal in writing to me along with the assignment and a copy of the syllabus. You and I then will meet to discuss the grade. Level 2: If you are still not satisfied, you may then appeal to the director of the School of Journalism. That appeal must be in writing and the response will be in writing. Level 3: If you are still not satisfied, you may submit your written documentation to the Dean of the Scripps College of Communication. The dean may deny the appeal or may appoint a committee to hear the appeal. The dean or the committee will also respond in writing.

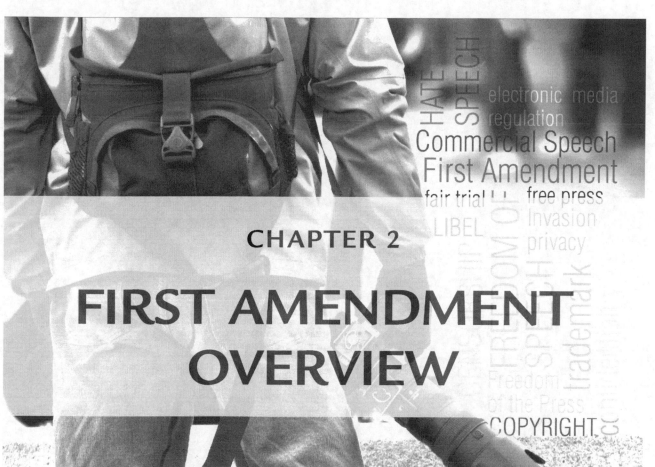

CHAPTER 2

FIRST AMENDMENT OVERVIEW

THE U.S. SYSTEM OF GOVENMENT

- Based on system of checks and balances
- Three estates or "branches" of government
- Media informally the "fourth" estate; the watchdog of government
- Free flow of information necessary for democracy to operate properly

SOURCES OF LAW

Billion Photos / Shutterstock.com

CONSTITUTIONAL

- Supreme law of land
- All other laws must be consistent with the Constitution
- Citizens have voice in changing constitution

STATUTORY

© Andrea Izzotti/Shutterstock.com

BRANCH	FEDERAL	STATE	LOCAL
LEGISLATIVE	Congress	State legislatures	City Council County Commission

ADMINISTRATIVE			
EXECUTIVE BRANCH	**FEDERAL**	**STATE**	**LOCAL**
	Departments Commissions Agencies	Departments Commissions Agencies	Departments Commissions Agencies

EXECUTIVE ORDERS

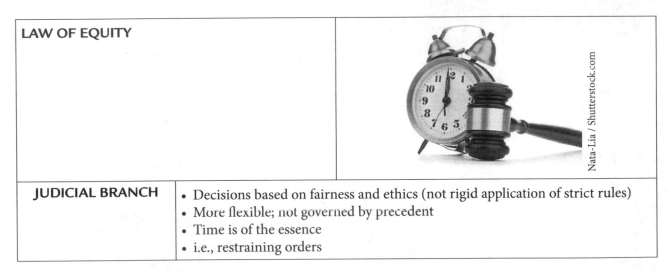

patrimonio designs ltd / Shutterstock.com

EXECUTIVE BRANCH	**FEDERAL**	**STATE**	**LOCAL**
	President	Governors	Mayors

LAW OF EQUITY

Nata-Lia / Shutterstock.com

JUDICIAL BRANCH	• Decisions based on fairness and ethics (not rigid application of strict rules) • More flexible; not governed by precedent • Time is of the essence • i.e., restraining orders

COMMON LAW OR CASE LAW

Brandon Bourdages / Shutterstock.com

JUDICIAL BRANCH	FEDERAL COURTS	STATE COURTS	LOCAL COURTS
	U.S. District Courts U.S. Courts of Appeals U.S. Supreme Courts Specialized federal courts	State trial courts State appeals courts State supreme courts	Municipal courts County Courts

SUPREME COURT OF THE UNITED STATES

John T Takai / Shutterstock.com

- Final arbiter on all legal questions involving U.S. Constitution and other federal and state laws
- Reviews decisions by U.S. Courts of Appeals and state supreme courts
- Comprised of Chief Justice of United States and eight associate justices
- Appointed by president with consent of the U.S. Senate
- Refer to textbook or credible web site for list of current Chief Justice and associate justices

urfin / Shutterstock.com

Religious and Political Freedom

Congress shall make no law respecting an establishment of religion, or prohibiting the free exercise thereof; or abridging the freedom of speech, or of the press; or the right of the people peaceably to assemble, and to petition the Government for a redress of grievances.

USCS Const. Amend. 1
Ratified December 15, 1791

Source: Washington, D.C., National Archives
http://www.archives.gov/exhibits/charters/bill_of_rights_transcript.html

THEORIES OF FREEDOM OF EXPRESSION

ABSOLUTIST THEORY

- <u>No</u> law means <u>no</u> law; <u>No</u> exceptions
- Speech and press have <u>absolute</u> protection from government interference
- Hugo L. Black (1937-1971); William O. Douglas (1939-1975)

Kriangx1234 / Shutterstock.com

AD HOC BALANCING THEORY

Glam / Shutterstock.com

- Freedom of speech and press only two of a number of important human rights
- Courts "balance" First Amendment with other government interests <u>equally</u> on a "case-by-case" basis
- "Scales" are erected anew in every case.

PREFERRED POSITION BALANCING THEORY

- First Amendment freedoms are fundamental to a free society
- First Amendment freedoms entitled to more judicial protection than other constitutional values
- Courts presume that government action limiting free speech/press is unconstitutional
- Government has burden of proof
- "Scales" tilted in favor of freedom of speech/press
- Easier to build a case in favor of broad interpretation of freedom of expression

Robert2301 / Shutterstock.com

MEIKLEJOHNIAN THEORY

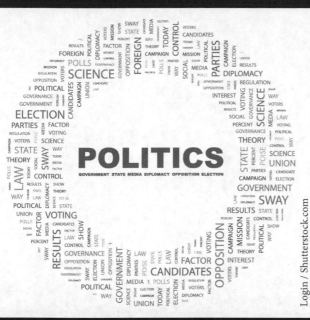

Login / Shutterstock.com

- Developed by philosopher Alexander Meiklejohn in the late 1940s
- Speech and press protected so that system of democracy can function
- Separates political speech from private speech
- Political speech has full First Amendment protection
- Private speech (i.e. obscenity, commercial speech, entertainment) can be regulated
- Critics argue line separating public (political) speech from private speech is not always clear
- Used by Supreme Court Justice William Brennan in development of actual malice test (libel law)

ACCESS THEORY

AlexDCentre / Shutterstock.com

- Developed in the mid-1960s
- Right of all people to have access to mass media
- Prompted by economic trends in nation
- Gives average citizen right to speak and publish— not just rich publishers
- First Amendment means more than simply right of wealthy and powerful to express their views
- Everyone else limited to passing out handbills or publishing small newsletters
- Media should be forced provide access to people with different points of view
- Courts apply this theory to broadcasting, cable and satellite
- Courts do not apply this theory to print

Chapter 2

FIRST AMENDMENT OVERVIEW: LIST OF CASES

- United States v. Alvarez, 132 S. Ct. 2537; 183 L. Ed. 2d 574 (2012)

CASE LAW NOTES TEMPLATE

(1) Description: What triggered the dispute; Who (full names and titles of plaintiffs; location; time frame) sued whom (full names and titles of defendants) and why (with specific examples/details). What were the plaintiff/appellee/petitioner's arguments? What were defendant/appellant/respondent's arguments?

(2) Resolution: Which court made the final decision; what the final court decision was (i.e., Who won and why; specific reasons how the court reached its decision (the court's rationale)

(3) Significance: What effect this court decision has had on this particular First Amendment issue?

(4) Application: How would you apply this court's rationale in this specific decision to future cases involving this same First Amendment issue (or to a hypothetical situation posed on your exam?

Wadim Wall / Shutterstock.com

CHAPTER 3

PRIOR RESTRAINT

Chapter 3

PRIOR RESTRAINT:

- New York Times v. U.S., 403 U.S. 713 (1971)

CASE LAW NOTES TEMPLATE

1. Description: What triggered the dispute; Who (full names and titles of plaintiffs; location; time frame) sued whom (full names and titles of defendants) and why (with specific examples/details). What were the plaintiff/appellee/petitioner's arguments? What were defendant/appellant/respondent's arguments?

2. Resolution: Which court made the final decision; what the final court decision was (i.e., Who won and why; specific reasons how the court reached its decision (the court's rationale)).

.3. Significance: What effect this court decision has had on this particular First Amendment issue?

4. Application: How would you apply this court's rationale in this specific decision to future cases involving this same First Amendment issue (or to a hypothetical situation posed on your exam?

Dawn Hudson / Shutterstock.com

Erika Cross / Shutterstock.com

PRIOR RESTRAINT/CLEAR AND PRESENT DANGER DOCTRINE

CONTROL OF INFORMATION IN ENGLAND	CONTROL OF INFORMATION IN THE UNITED STATES
• Seditious Libel • Licensing • Bonding	• Alien and Sedition Acts (1798) • Espionage Act (1917) • Smith Act (1940) • USA Patriot Act (2001)

ALIEN AND SEDITION ACTS 1798

- Designed to silence political dissent; aimed at opponents of President Adams
- Alien Act controlled immigration
- Sedition Act made it a federal crime to speak or publish seditious ideas; expired in 1801
- Fine of $2,000 or two years in prison
- About 25 arrests; 15 indictments

ESPIONAGE ACT (1917)

- Passed shortly after U.S. entered World War I (amended with the Sedition Act of 1918)
- 1917 Espionage Act still on the books today; 1918 Sedition Act expired
- Congress desired to suppress unpopular views; vigorously enforced; 2,000 arrested
- Example: Grandmother arrested for writing a letter to grandson not to join the army
- *Schenck v. United States* (1919)

CLEAR AND PRESENT DANGER DOCTRINE

- Speech must cause danger
- Danger must be immediate
- Danger must be grave/serious

SMITH ACT (1940)

- Peacetime sedition act; passed before U.S. entered World War II
- Crime to advocate forceful overthrow of government or to "recruit" members for groups with goal to overthrow government
- Applied during peace time as well as during war; enforced during "Cold War" after WWII
- Used to prosecute members of American Communist Party during "Red Scare" of 1950s (McCarthyism)
- *Dennis v. U.S.* (1951); *Yates v. U.S.* (1957)

Chapter 3

PRIOR RESTRAINT: LIST OF CASES

- Schneck v. U.S., 249 U.S. 47 (1919)
- Near v. Minnesota, 283 U.S. 697 (1931)
- New York Times v. U.S., 403 U.S. 713 (1971)

CASE LAW NOTES TEMPLATE

1. Description: What triggered the dispute; Who (full names and titles of plaintiffs; location; time frame) sued whom (full names and titles of defendants) and why (with specific examples/details). What were the plaintiff/appellee/petitioner's arguments? What were defendant/appellant/respondent's arguments?

2. Resolution: Which court made the final decision? What the final court decision was (i.e., who won and why; specific reasons how the court reached its decision (the court's rationale))?

3. Significance: What effect this court decision has had on this particular First Amendment issue?

4. Application: How would you apply this court's rationale in this specific decision to future cases involving this same First Amendment issue (or to a hypothetical situation posed on your exam)?

Alias Ching / Shutterstock.com

CHAPTER 4

STUDENTS & STUDENT MEDIA

Chapter 4

STUDENTS & STUDENT MEDIA: LIST OF CASES

- Tinker v. Des Moines Independent Community School District, 393 U.S. 503 (1969)
- Bethel School District v Fraser, 478 U.S. 675 (1986)
- Hazelwood v. Kuhlmeier, 484 U.S. 260 (1988)
- Morse v. Frederick, 551 U.S. 393 (2007)
- Harper v. Poway Unified Sch. Dist., 445 F. 3d 1166 (9th Cir 2006)

CASE LAW NOTES TEMPLATE

1. Description: What triggered the dispute; Who (full names and titles of plaintiffs; location; time frame) sued whom (full names and titles of defendants) and why (with specific examples/details). What were the plaintiff/appellee/petitioner's arguments? What were defendant/appellant/respondent's arguments?

2. Resolution: Which court made the final decision? What the final court decision was (i.e., who won and why; specific reasons how the court reached its decision (the court's rationale))?

3. Significance: What effect this court decision has had on this particular First Amendment issue?

4. Application: How would you apply this court's rationale in this specific decision to future cases involving this same First Amendment issue (or to a hypothetical situation posed on your exam)?

GraphicsRF / Shutterstock.com

Chapter 4

STUDENTS & THE INTERNET: LIST OF CASES

- Bell v. Itawamba County School Board, 799 F. 3d 379, 2015 U.S. App. LEXIS 14630, (5th Cir. Miss, 2015)
- Burge v. Colton School District, 100 F. Supp. 3d 1057; 2015 U.S. Dist. LEXIS 51596 (U.S. Dist. Oregon, 2015)
- C.R. v. Eugene School District, 2016 U.S. App. LEXIS 16202 (9th Cir, 2016)

CASE LAW NOTES TEMPLATE

1. Description: What triggered the dispute; Who (full names and titles of plaintiffs; location; time frame) sued whom (full names and titles of defendants) and why (with specific examples/details). What were the plaintiff/appellee/petitioner's arguments? What were defendant/appellant/respondent's arguments?

2. Resolution: Which court made the final decision? What the final court decision was (i.e., who won and why; specific reasons how the court reached its decision (the court's rationale))?

3. Significance: What effect this court decision has had on this particular First Amendment issue?

4. Application: How would you apply this court's rationale in this specific decision to future cases involving this same First Amendment issue (or to a hypothetical situation posed on your exam?

gcpics / Shutterstock.com

Chapter 4

COLLEGE MEDIA: LIST OF CASES

- Hosty v. Carter, 2005 U.S. App. LEXIS 11761 (7th Cir IL 2005)
- Kincaid v. Gibson, 236 F. 3d 342 (6th Cir OH 2001)

CASE LAW NOTES TEMPLATE

1 Description: What triggered the dispute; Who (full names and titles of plaintiffs; location; time frame) sued whom (full names and titles of defendants) and why (with specific examples/details). What were the plaintiff/appellee/petitionerís arguments? What were defendant/appellant/respondentís arguments?

2. Resolution: Which court made the final decision? What the final court decision was (i.e., who won and why; specific reasons how the court reached its decision (the courtís rationale))?

3. Significance: What effect this court decision has had on this particular First Amendment issue?

4. Application: How would you apply this courtís rationale in this specific decision to future cases involving this same First Amendment issue (or to a hypothetical situation posed on your exam)?

CHAPTER 5

HATE SPEECH & SYMBOLIC SPEECH

SYMBOLIC SPEECH & HATE SPEECH

First Amendment
- Freedom of speech
- Freedom of the press
- Freedom of to assemble

Yulia Glam / Shutterstock.com

Fourteenth Amendment
- Equal protection under the law
- Equal rights
- Safety

TYPES OF SPEECH

- Pure speech: verbal or written
- "Speech plus": speech + conduct; communicating ideas via language & action (behavior); <u>**symbolic speech**</u>

GOVERNMENT CONTROL OF SPEECH

- Content-based laws: presumed invalid; strict scrutiny; i.e., injunctions (restraining orders) to prevent publication
- Content-neutral laws: do not discriminate on basis of content; time/manner/place (TMP); intermediate-<u>scrutiny;</u> i.e., noise ordinances; laws prohibiting burning of draft cards

O'BRIEN TEST (1968)	BRANDENBURG TEST (1969)
1. Government has constitutional authority 2. Needed to further important/ substantial government interest 3. **Content neutral** 4. Prohibits no more speech than necessary to further interest	Government may punish criticism or advocacy of radical ideas **only** when that speech is: 1. Directed toward intentionally inciting 2. Immediate violence or illegal action & 3. Is likely to produce that action

HATE SPEECH	HATE CRIMES
- Negative verbal and written words or symbolic acts - Attack race, gender, ethnicity, religion, sexual orientation or disability - Language is typically coarse - Purpose is to humiliate or wound **NOT** to communicate ideas	- Acts of violence motivated by hatred based on race, religion, national origin, gender or sexual orientation

FIRST AMENDMENT PROTECTION

PROTECTED	NOT PROTECTED
"Rhetorical hyperbole" Hate speech Wearing black armbands to school to protest the war Cross burning (i.e., KKK rally) Burning U.S. flag to protest the war Swastikas	"Fighting Words" Doctrine Hate crimes Wearing anti-gay T-shirt to school Cross burning as form of intimidation Burning draft cards to protest the war

St. Paul Hate Crime Law

Ruled **unconstitutional** by U.S. Supreme Court in R.A.V. v. St. Paul (1992)

Whoever places on public or private property a symbol, object, appellation, characterization or graffiti, including but not limited to, a burning cross or Nazi swastika, which one knows or has reasonable grounds to know arouses anger, alarm or resentment in others on the basis of race, color, creed, religion or gender commits disorderly conduct and shall be guilty of a misdemeanor.

Wisconsin Hate Crime law

Ruled constitutional by U.S. Supreme Court in Wisconsin v. Mitchell (1993)

Wis. Stat. § 939.645 (2003) Penalty; crimes committed against certain people or property.

(1) If a person does all of the following, the penalties for the underlying crime are increased as provided in sub.

(2): (a) Commits a crime under chs. 939 to 948

(b) Intentionally selects the person against whom the crime under par.

(a) is committed or selects the property that is damaged or otherwise affected by the crime under par.

(a) in whole or in part because of the actors belief or perception regarding the race, religion, color, disability, sexual orientation, national origin or ancestry of that person or the owner or occupant of that property, whether or not the actors belief or perception was correct.

(3) This section provides for the enhancement of the penalties applicable for the underlying crime.

Virginia Anti-Cross Burning Law

Ruled constitutional by U.S. Supreme Court in Black v. Virginia (2003)

Va. Code Ann. § 18.2-423 (2004) Burning cross on property of another or public place with intent to intimidate; penalty; prima facie evidence of intent

It shall be unlawful for any person or persons, with the intent of intimidating any person or group of persons, to burn, or cause to be burned, a cross on the property of another, a highway or other public place. Any person who shall violate any provision of this section shall be guilty of a Class 6 felony.

Any such burning of a cross shall be prima facie evidence of an intent to intimidate a person or group of persons.

Florida Anti-Cross Burning law

Ruled constitutional by State Supreme Court of Florida (1995); U.S. Supreme Court denied cert (1996)

Fla. Stat. § 876.18 (2004) Placing burning or flaming cross on property of another

It shall be unlawful for any person or persons to place or cause to be placed on the property of another in the state a burning or flaming cross or any manner of exhibit in which a burning or flaming cross, real or simulated, is a whole or part without first obtaining written permission of the owner or occupier of the premises to so do. Any person who violates this section commits a misdemeanor of the first degree, punishable as provided in s. 775.082 or s. 775.083.

Ohio Hate Crime law

§ 2927.12. Ethnic intimidation

(A) No person shall violate section 2903.21, 2903.22, 2909.06, or 2909.07, or division (A)(3), (4), or (5) of section 2917.21 of the Revised Code by reason of the race, color, religion, or national origin of another person or group of persons.

(B) Whoever violates this section is guilty of ethnic intimidation. Ethnic intimidation is an offense of the next higher degree than the offense the commission of which is a necessary element of ethnic intimidation.

Chapter 5

HATE SPEECH & SYMBOLIC SPEECH: LIST OF CASES

- U.S. v. O'Brien, 391 U.S.367 (1968)
- Cohen v. California, 403 U.S. 15 (1971)
- Chaplinsky v. New Hampshire, 315 U.S. 528 (1942)
- Brandenburg v. Ohio, 395 U.S.444 (1969)
- Texas v. Johnson, 491 U.S. 397 (1989)
- U.S. v. Eichman, 496 U.S. 310 (1990)
- Phelps v. Powers, 2014 U.S. Dist. LEXIS 167825 (US SD Iowa, December 3, 2014)
- Virginia v. Black, 2003 U.S. LEXIS 2715 (2003)
- Wisconsin v. Mitchell, 508 U.S. 476 (1993)
- Walker v. Texas Division, Sons of the Confederate Veterans, Inc., 2015 U.S. LEXIS 4063 (2015)

Sergey Kamshylin / Shutterstock.com

CASE LAW NOTES TEMPLATE

1. Description: What triggered the dispute; Who (full names and titles of plaintiffs; location; time frame) sued whom (full names and titles of defendants) and why (with specific examples/details). What were the plaintiff/appellee/petitioner's arguments? What were defendant/appellant/respondent's arguments?

2. Resolution: Which court made the final decision? What the final court decision was (i.e., who won and why; specific reasons how the court reached its decision (the court's rationale))?

3. Significance: What effect this court decision has had on this particular First Amendment issue?

4. Application: How would you apply this court's rationale in this specific decision to future cases involving this same First Amendment issue (or to a hypothetical situation posed on your exam)?

Stefano Panzeri / Shutterstock.com

Omelianenko Anna / Shutterstock.com

Alan Uster / Shutterstock.com

Timothy R. Nichols / Shutterstock.com

John T Takai / Shutterstock.com

CHAPTER 6

LIBEL (DEFAMATION)

LIBEL LAW OVERVIEW

TWO TYPES OF DEFAMATION

- Slander
- **Libel**

TWO FORMS OF LIBEL

- Libel per se
- Libel per quod

ABSOLUTE DEFENSES (100% protection)

- Truth

  "Truth is generally the best vindication against slander." —*Abraham Lincoln*

- Consent
- Statute of Limitations
- Privilege

QUALIFIED DEFENSES (some protection; no guarantees)

- Actual Malice Test
- Neutral Reportage/Fair <u>Report</u>
- Opinion/Fair <u>Comment</u>
- Safe Harbor

OTHER RELATED ISSUES/JARGON

- Summary Judgment
- Writ of certiorari (i.e., "denied cert"; "cert granted")
- "Chilling Effect"
- "Slippery Slope"
- Retraction
- Intentional Infliction of Emotional Harm/Distress
- SLAPP (Strategic Lawsuit Against Public Participation)
- SPEECH Act 2010/Libel Tourism

OHIO REVISED CODE: DEFINITION OF PUBLIC OFFICIAL*	
Ohio	**ORC ANN. 102.01**
	(B) "Public official or employee" means any person who is elected or appointed to an office or is an employee of any public agency. "Public official or employee" does not include a person elected or appointed to the office of precinct, ward, or district committee member under section 3517.03 of the Revised Code, any presidential elector, or any delegate to a national convention. "Public official or employee" does not include a person who is a teacher, instructor, professor, or other kind of educator whose position does not involve the performance of, or authority to perform, administrative or supervisory functions.

	ORC ANN. 2921.01
	Definitions As used in sections 2921.01 to 2921.45 of the Revised Code: (A) "Public official" means any elected or appointed officer, or employee, or agent of the state or any political subdivision, whether in a temporary or permanent capacity, and includes, but is not limited to, legislators, judges, and law enforcement officers. © Lawriter LLC. Reprinted by permission.

ACTUAL MALICE

- Published with knowledge of falsity
- Published with reckless disregard for the truth or falsity
- Published with serious doubts that the statements were true
- Public officials and public figures must prove actual malice in order to win a libel suit
- Actual malice standard applies only if libel dispute pertains to the plaintiff's official conduct or "general fitness for office"

ACTUAL MALICE TEST CRITERIA

- Was there deadline pressure? Was there time to investigate the story or did the story have to be published quickly?
- Was the source of the information reliable and trustworthy?
- Did the story sound probable or farfetched?

PROVING ACTUAL MALICE (for public officials/figures)

- Plaintiff has burden of proof of falsity of story
- Plaintiff must prove falsity by "clear and convincing evidence"
- Plaintiff can ask questions about media defendant's state of mind during the editorial process

Knowing Falsehood
• Media defendant simply fabricates defamatory "facts" out of thin air

Reckless Disregard
• Story based wholly on unverified information from an anonymous telephone call or from an unreliable source • Deliberate decision not to acquire knowledge of facts that might confirm the falsity of the story
• Purposeful avoidance of the truth • More than just simple failure to investigate • More than just sloppy or unethical journalistic practices

PROVING NEGLIGENCE (for private figures)

- Required of private figure plaintiffs who sue the media for libel
- Failure to exercise "reasonable care"
- Failure to take the precautions that a reasonable communicator would have taken under similar circumstances to assure that libelous communications were not disseminated.
- Far lesser degree of fault than actual malice
- Adequacy of efforts to verify information
- NOT necessary that all avenues of verification possible be exhausted in every case

LIBEL PLAINTIFF: FOUR CATEGORIES

1. Public Officials
2. General Purpose Public Figures
3. Limited Purpose Public Figures
4. Private Figures

PUBLIC OFFICIALS

- Government employees with substantial responsibility for or control over the conduct of government affairs
- Have opportunities to contradict a lie or correct the error to minimize its adverse impact on reputation
- Have greater access to effective media communication to correct mistakes
- Does NOT apply to everyone who receives a government paycheck
- NOT reserved exclusively for the very highest levels of government
- Examples: elected or appointed representatives, high-ranking officers in the armed forces, judges, prosecutors, public defenders, sheriffs, police officers
- New York Times v. Sullivan (1964)

"GENERAL PURPOSE" PUBLIC FIGURES

- Have assumed roles of special prominence in the affairs of society
- Have voluntarily thrust themselves into the forefront of particular public controversies in order to influence the resolution of the issues involved
- Invite public attention and public comment

- Occupy positions of such persuasive power and influence that they are deemed public figures for all purposes
- "Household names"—internationally, nationally, or regionally where the defamatory content was published
- Examples: nationally known film stars (i.e., Clint Eastwood, Tom Cruise, Samuel L. Jackson); celebrities/ entertainers (i.e., Bill Cosby, Brittany Spears, Michael Jackson, Jim Carrey, Jerry Seinfeld, Brittany Spears, Mary-Kate and Ashley Olson); professional sports figures (i.e., tennis champions Serena Williams or Svetlana Kuznetsova; Los Angeles Lakers Kobe Bryant and Shaquille O'Neal), or big name social critics (i.e., political activist and sometime presidential candidate Ralph Nader, filmmaker Michael Moore)
- Curtis v. Butts/AP v. Walker (1967)

According to one federal judge, defining a public figure is like "trying to nail a jellyfish to the wall."

"LIMITED PURPOSE" PUBLIC FIGURES

- Have entered the public spotlight, but only within a narrow context (i.e., one particular issue)
- Plaintiffs are considered "limited purpose" public figures only if the defamation was related to that public context
- Examples: lobbyists, union leaders, vocal abortion rights advocates
- Court decision on whether plaintiff is public figure based on actual, voluntary involvement in public debate that triggered the libel suit
- Gertz v. Welch (1974); Jewell v. Atlanta Journal-Constitution (2001)

PRIVATE FIGURES

- Individuals who do not meet the definition of either a public official or a public figure
- More vulnerable to injury; therefore, more protection from the courts
- Only need to prove negligence—not actual malice—to win a libel suit

Chapter 6

LIBEL (ABSOLUTE DEFENSES): LIST OF CASES

- Nichols v. Moore, 477 F.3d 396 (6th Cir 2007)
- Clark v. Viacom, 43 Med. L. Rep. 2029 (6th Circuit, 2015)
- Hutchinson v. Proxmire, 443 U.S. 111 (1979)

CASE LAW NOTES TEMPLATE

1. Description: What triggered the dispute? Who (full names and titles of plaintiffs; location; time frame) sued whom (full names and titles of defendants) and why (with specific examples/details)? What were the plaintiff/appellee/petitioner's arguments? What were defendant/appellant/respondent's arguments?

2. Resolution: Which court made the final decision? What the final court decision was (i.e., who won and why; specific reasons how the court reached its decision (the court's rationale))?

3. Significance: What effect this court decision has had on this particular First Amendment issue?

4. Application: How would you apply this court's rationale in this specific decision to future cases involving this same First Amendment issue (or to a hypothetical situation posed on your exam)?

Chapter 6

LIBEL (ACTUAL MALICE TEST): LIST OF CASES

- New York Times v. Sullivan, 376 U.S. 254 (1964)
- Curtis Pub. Co. v. Butts/Associated Press v. Walker, 388 U.S. 130, 87 S. Ct. 1975 (1967)
- Atlanta Journal Constitution v. Jewell, 251 Ga. App. 808 (2001)

CASE LAW NOTES TEMPLATE

1. Description: What triggered the dispute? Who (full names and titles of plaintiffs; location; time frame) sued whom (full names and titles of defendants) and why (with specific examples/details)? What were the plaintiff/appellee/petitioner's arguments? What were defendant/appellant/respondent's arguments?

2. Resolution: Which court made the final decision? What the final court decision was (i.e., who won and why; specific reasons how the court reached its decision (the court's rationale))?

3. Significance: What effect this court decision has had on this particular First Amendment issue?

4. Application: How would you apply this court's rationale in this specific decision to future cases involving this same First Amendment issue (or to a hypothetical situation posed on your exam)?

Chapter 6

LIBEL (OTHER DEFENSES): LIST OF CASES

- Milkovich v. Lorain Journal, 497 U.S. 1 (1990)
- Scholz v. Boston Herald, 41 N.E. 3d 38 (Mass Sup Ct, 2015)
- Jones v. Dirty World Entertainment Recordings, 840 F. Supp. 2d 1008; 2012 U.S. Dist. LEXIS 2525 (2012)

CASE LAW NOTES TEMPLATE

1. Description: What triggered the dispute? Who (full names and titles of plaintiffs; location; time frame) sued whom (full names and titles of defendants) and why (with specific examples/details)? What were the plaintiff/appellee/petitioner's arguments? What were defendant/appellant/respondent's arguments?

2. Resolution: Which court made the final decision? What the final court decision was (i.e., who won and why; specific reasons how the court reached its decision (the court's rationale))?

3. Significance: What effect this court decision has had on this particular First Amendment issue?

4. Application: How would you apply this court's rationale in this specific decision to future cases involving this same First Amendment issue (or to a hypothetical situation posed on your exam)?

Chapter 6
LIBEL (RELATED ISSUES): LIST OF CASES

- Hustler v. Falwell, 485 U.S. 46 (1988)
- Levitt v. Felton (Mich slip opinion, 2015)

CASE LAW NOTES TEMPLATE

1. Description: What triggered the dispute? Who (full names and titles of plaintiffs; location; time frame) sued whom (full names and titles of defendants) and why (with specific examples/details)? What were the plaintiff/appellee/petitioner's arguments? What were defendant/appellant/respondent's arguments?

2. Resolution: Which court made the final decision? What the final court decision was (i.e., who won and why; specific reasons how the court reached its decision (the court's rationale))?

3. Significance: What effect this court decision has had on this particular First Amendment issue?

4. Application: How would you apply this court's rationale in this specific decision to future cases involving this same First Amendment issue (or to a hypothetical situation posed on your exam)?

s_bukley / Shutterstock.com

Jeff Fusco/Stringer/Getty

CHAPTER 7

INVASION OF PRIVACY

PRIVACY

Four Types
1. Appropriation/Right of Publicity
2. Intrusion
3. Private Facts
4. False Light

Appropriation
- Using a person's name or likeness without permission for commercial gain

Two Types
1. Commercialization
2. Right of Publicity

COMMERCIALIZATION	RIGHT OF PUBLICITY
- Using a (private) person's name, likeness, voice - For advertising or other commercial uses - Without permission **Defenses:** - Newsworthiness - Incidental use - Advertising for a mass medium - Consent	- Right to control commercial use of individual's likeness/identity **Defense:** - Consent or Transformation

Intrusion
- "Keyhole" journalism
- Invading a person's solitude

Defense:
- Newsworthiness

Three Types:
1. Possession of stolen property
2. Newsgathering
3. Trespass

Defense:
- Newsworthiness

iQoncept / Shutterstock.com

Private Facts
- Publication of true BUT personal, intimate information
- Not of legitimate public concern
- Highly offensive to reasonable person

Defense:
- Newsworthiness

False Light
- "First cousin" to libel
- Publication that leaves false impression (good or bad)
- Highly offensive to a reasonable person
- Not recognized in all states

Defense:
- Actual Malice

Chapter 7

PRIVACY: LIST OF CASES

- Carson v. Here's Johnny, 698 F.2d 831 (6th Cir 1983)
- In Re NCAA Student-Athlete Name & Likeness Licensing Litigation, 724 F. 3d 1268 (9th Cir, July 2013)
- Bullard v. MRA Holding, 292 Ga. 748; 740 S.E.2d 622 (Sup. Ct. GA, 2013)
- Snyder v. Phelps, 131 S. Ct. 1207(2011)
- Showler v. Harper's Magazine Foundation, 2007 U.S. App. LEXIS 7025 (10th Cir 2007)
- Bollea v. Gawker (trial court decision, March 2016)
- Solano v. Playgirl, Inc., 2002 U.S. App. LEXIS 11437 (9th Cir 2002)

CASE LAW NOTES TEMPLATE

1. Description: What triggered the dispute? Who (full names and titles of plaintiffs; location; time frame) sued whom (full names and titles of defendants) andwhy (with specific examples/details)? What were the plaintiff/appellee/petitioner's arguments? What were defendant/appellant/respondent's arguments?

2. Resolution: Which court made the final decision? What the final court decision was (i.e., who won and why; specific reasons how the court reached its decision (the court's rationale))?

3. Significance: What effect this court decision has had on this particular First Amendment issue?

4. Application: How would you apply this court's rationale in this specific decision to future casesinvolving this same First Amendment issue (or to a hypothetical situation posed on your exam)?

CHAPTER 8

ELECTRONIC MEDIA, VIDEO GAMES & THE INTERNET

THREE APPROACHES TOWARD MEDIA REGUALTION

1. Marketplace Approach
   - Example: print
   - Let economic forces control content—not government
2. Common Carrier Approach
   - Examples: telephony, telegraph
   - Does not create original programming (e.g., editorials, talk shows, soap operas, movies, etc.)
   - Content-neutral regulation
   - No government content regulation needed
3. Public Trusteeship Approach
   - Example: Broadcasting (over-the-air): radio and TV
   - Government regulates content in the public interest

WHY THE GOVERNMENT REGULATES BROADCASTING

- Spectrum scarcity
- Licensing
- Limited frequencies
"Public Interest, Necessity and Convenience"
- Airwaves: a public resource like parks and rivers
- Fear
- Effect on children
- Pervasiveness; constantly intrusive

xzoex / Shutterstock.com

FEDERAL COMMUNICATIONS COMMISSION

- Government agency created by Congress
- Communications Act of 1934
- Mandate: To regulate broadcasting in "public interest, necessity & convenience"
- "Traffic cop of the airwaves"
- Authority includes **content** regulation
- Its decisions are "administrative law"

POLITICAL BROADCASTING REGULATIONS

Section 312 (Communications Act of 1934)
- **Must** provide "reasonable access" to candidates in **federal** elections
- No such obligation for state & local offices
- Violation could result in loss of license

Section 315 (Communications Act of 1934)
- Equal Time rule or "equal opportunity provision"
- Equal (but not free) access to all legally qualified candidates
- Exempts "bona fide" newscasts, news interviews, news events, talk shows, etc.
- Equal access: "all" or "none"
- Violation could result in loss of license

a Sk / Shutterstock.com

EdgeOfReason / Shutterstock.com

FAIRNESS DOCTRINE

- FCC **policy** (1949-1987); officially eliminated August 2011

Broadcast license holders **required** to:
- Cover important issues to public
- Provide multiple perspectives on issues of public importance
- Includes: Personal Attack Rule
- Red Lion v. FCC (1969)
- Miami Herald v. Tornillo (1974)

MUST CARRY

- Cable Television Consumer Protection and Competition Act of 1992 (Cable Act) [sections 4 & 5]
- required cable television systems to dedicate some of their channels to local broadcast television stations.
- designed to serve three interrelated, important governmental interests:
    1. preserving benefits of free, over the air local broadcast television,
    2. promoting widespread dissemination of information from a multiple of sources
    3. promoting fair competition in TV programming market.
- Broadcasters loved "must carry"; cable TV operators did **not**.
- Turner v. FCC (Turner 1, 1994); Turner v. FCC (Turner II, 1997)

" *[T]he Internet may fairly be regarded as a never-ending worldwide conversation. The Government may not, through the CDA, interrupt that conversation . . . As most participatory form of mass speech yet developed, the Internet deserves the highest protection from government intrusion.*"

—ACLU v. Reno (ED. Pa. 1996)

INTERNET & LIBEL

1. Single Publication Rule
2. Jurisdiction
3. Safe Harbor
    - Congress, within the Communication Decency Act, created a "safe harbor" for Internet providers:

Mmaxer / Shutterstock.com

Section 230 defines an "interactive computer service" as "any information service system or access software provider that provides or enables computer access to multiple users to a computer server including specifically a service or system that provides access to the Internet . . ."

47 U.S.C. § 230(f)(2).

As a result, Internet providers
- Cannot be treated as publishers
- Cannot be held responsible for information for which they do **not** have editorial control

---

"*Some of the dialogue on the Internet surely tests the limits of conventional discourse. Speech on the Internet can be unfiltered, unpolished, and unconventional, even emotionally charged, sexually explicit, and vulgar in a word, "indecent" in many communities. But we should expect such speech to occur in a medium in which citizens from all walks of life have a voice.*" From:

DiMeo v. Tucker (2006)

BROWN V. ENTERTAINMENT MERCHANTS ASSOCIATION (2011)

Key Issues:
- First time **interactive medium** before U.S. Supreme Court
- Can government regulate children's access to violent video games?
- Can violence (like obscenity) be considered unprotected speech?
- How do you draw the line? Should you?
- Should "violent content" become a new category of content regulation?

RANK ORDER OF FIRST AMENDMENT PROTECTION

Most Protection:
- Political speech
- Ideas; Opinions; Hate speech; Symbolic speech
- Print media; Internet; **Video games**

Some Protection:
- **Cable**

Less Protection:
- **Broadcast media**
- Commercial speech
- Pornography; **indecency**

Even Less Protection
- Advertising for legal—but harmful—products, i.e., tobacco, gambling, alcohol

No Protection:
- False facts about individuals, products, or businesses
- Fighting words; hate crimes
- Obscenity; child pornography
- False advertising

BROADCAST INDECENCY

Federal law bans the broadcast of "any obscene, indecent, or profane language."

Title 18 U. S. C. ß1464

Obscenity

- No First Amendment protection; no adult access at all in any medium
- Includes child pornography
- Miller v. California (1973)
- Ohio's obscenity Law: Ohio Revised Code 2907.31-2907.37

"The Miller Test"

- An average person, applying <u>contemporary community standards</u> would find that the work, <u>taken as a whole</u>, appeals to the prurient interest.
- The work depicts or describes, in a patently offensive way, sexual conduct specifically defined by the applicable state law.
- The work, taken as a whole, lacks serious literary, artistic, political, or scientific value.

Pornography

- Some First Amendment protection
- Adult access only
- Efforts to ban pornography that contain violence against women (i.e., rape, degradation, exploitation, humiliation)
- American Booksellers v. Hudnut (1986)

Dr. D.'S Definition Of Pornography

A work (video, audio, book, magazine, photograph) that contains descriptions of sexual conduct **but** does have <u>**some**</u> (a "tad"; a "smidgen"; "just enough to convince a jury it's not legally obscene) serious literary, artistic, political, or scientific value.

Indecency

- Most First Amendment protection in print media
- Regulated in broadcast media to "safe harbor" period when children are least likely to hear it.
- "filthy words" you should not say in "front of the kids"

"The ease in with which children may obtain access to broadcast material . . . justifies special treatment of indecent broadcasting."

—John Paul Stevens, U.S. Supreme Court justice, *FCC v. Pacifica*, 1978

FCC's Definition Of Indecency

"Language that describes in terms patently offensive as measured by contemporary community standards for the broadcast medium, sexual or excretory activities and organs, at times of day when there is a reasonable risk children may be in the audience."

BeRad / Shutterstock.com

Chapter 8

ELECTRONIC MEDIA & VIDEO GAMES: LIST OF CASES

- Red Lion Broadcasting Co. v. FCC, 395 U.S. 367 (1969)
- Citizens United v. Federal Elections Commission, 130 S. Ct. 876; 175 L. Ed. 2d 753 (2010)
- Turner v. FCC, 520 U.S. 180 (1997)
- FCC v. Pacifica, 438 U.S. 726 (1978)
- FCC v. Fox TV Stations, Inc./FCC v. ABC, Inc., 132 S. Ct. 2307, 183 L. Ed. 2d 234 (2012)
- CBS Corp. v. FCC, 663 F. 3d 122, 2011 U.S. App. LEXIS 22501 (3d Cir. 2011)

CASE LAW NOTES TEMPLATE

1. Description: What triggered the dispute? Who (full names and titles of plaintiffs; location; time frame) sued whom (full names and titles of defendants) and why (with specific examples/details)? What were the plaintiff/appellee/petitioner's arguments? What were defendant/appellant/respondent's arguments?

2. Resolution: Which court made the final decision? What the final court decision was (i.e., who won and why; specific reasons how the court reached its decision (the court's rationale))?

3. Significance: What effect this court decision has had on this particular First Amendment issue?

4. Application: How would you apply this court's rationale in this specific decision to future cases involving this same First Amendment issue (or to a hypothetical situation posed on your exam)?

Chapter 8

INTERNET: LIST OF CASES

- Reno v. ACLU, 521 U.S. 844 (1997)
- Bland v. Roberts, 2013 U.S. App. LEXIS 19268 (4th Cir, 2013)
- Noah v. AOL-Time Warner, 261 F. Supp. 2d 532 (US Dist. E. VA 2003)
- Elonis v. U.S., 135 S.Ct. 2001 (2015)
- Brown v. Entertainment Merchants Association, 131 S. Ct. 2729, 180 L. Ed. 2d 708 (2011)

beboy / Shutterstock.com

CASE LAW NOTES TEMPLATE

1. Description: What triggered the dispute? Who (full names and titles of plaintiffs; location; time frame) sued whom (full names and titles of defendants) and why (with specific examples/details)? What were the plaintiff/appellee/petitioner's arguments? What were defendant/appellant/respondent's arguments?

2. Resolution: Which court made the final decision; what the final court decision was (i.e., who won and why; specific reasons how the court reached its decision (the court's rationale))?

3. Significance: What effect this court decision has had on this particular First Amendment issue?

4. Application: How would you apply this court's rationale in this specific decision to future cases involving this same First Amendment issue (or to a hypothetical situation posed on your exam)?

Sarawut Aiemsinsuk / Shutterstock.com

CHAPTER 9

ACCESS TO
INFORMATION

Freedom of Information Act (1966)
5 USCS § 552 (2004)

The U.S. Freedom of Information Act (FOIA) is a law ensuring public access to U.S. government records. FOIA carries a presumption of disclosure; the burden is on the government—not the public—to substantiate why information may not be released. Upon written request, agencies of the United States government are required to disclose those records, unless they can be lawfully withheld from disclosure under one of nine specific exemptions in the FOIA. This right of access is ultimately enforceable in federal court. The full text of this law can be found at http://www.justice.gov/oip/amended-foia-redlined.pdf.

The act explicitly applies only to executive branch government agencies. (Congress is exempt from having to comply with the very law it passed. Also, FOIA include nine exemptions that a government agency (i.e., FBI, Department of Agriculture, IRS, etc.) can use to prevent the release of certain information that agency has in its files:

Nine Exemptions to FOIA

1. National Security
2. Internal Personnel and Practices
   - "Housekeeping" (i.e., parking lot assignments, vacation schedules; the office "coffee pot" fund)
   - Material of little or no public concern; routine matters of "merely internal significance"
   - Disclosure of this type of information would unduly burden agencies
3. Statutes
   - Privacy Act of 1974
   - Family Education Rights and Privacy Act (FERPA or "Buckley Amendment")
4. Trade Secrets/Financial or Commercial Information
5. Executive Privilege
   - Legal foundation is vague
   - Covers military and diplomatic secrets
   - Also includes internal documents generated within the executive branch (i.e., working papers, tentative drafts)
   - Used by executive officers at federal, state and local levels
   - Executive privilege absolute only for military or diplomatic information to protect national security
   - In other areas, executive privilege must be balanced with other interests. Like reporter's privilege (in libel law), executive privilege has limitations,
6. Personnel and Medical Files and "similar" documents
7. Law Enforcement Investigation: files that would:
   - Interfere with law enforcement or deprive person of a fair trial
   - Unwarranted invasion of personal privacy
   - Disclose confidential source or endanger life or safety of any individual

- Disclose techniques to help someone circumvent the law
8. Records of Financial Institutions
   - Financial reports, audits, and mandatory filing information provided to the federal government by banks, credit unions, trust companies and other financial institutions.
   - Designed to protect the stability of (and the public's faith in) the banking system
9. Drilling Information
   - Maps, descriptions and geological data related to the locations of natural resources (oil, natural gas and water)

The Privacy Act of 1974

Citation: The Privacy Act of 1974, 5 U.S.C. § 552a, Public Law No. 93-579, (Dec. 31, 1974).

The Privacy Act of 1974 (as amended) governs the collection, maintenance, use, and dissemination of personally identifiable information about individuals that is maintained by federal agencies (i.e., IRS, SEC, FTC, FBI).

> "No agency shall disclose any record which is contained in a system of records by any means of communication to any person, or to another agency, except pursuant to a written request by, or with the prior written consent of, the individual to whom the record pertains. . ."

The Privacy Act also provides for individuals to have access to information a government agency may have about them:

- Each agency that maintains a system of records shall—upon request by any individual . . . permit him . . . to review the record and have a copy made of all or any portion thereof in a form comprehensible to him . . .
- permit the individual to request amendment of a record pertaining to him . . .

The Privacy Act also has specific exceptions allowing the government's use of personal records:

- For statistical purposes by the Census Bureau and the Bureau of Labor Statistics
- For routine uses within a U.S. government agency
- For archival purposes "as a record which has sufficient historical or other value to warrant its continued preservation by the United States Government"
- For law enforcement purposes
- For congressional investigations
- Other administrative purposes

The Privacy Act mandates that each United States Government agency have in place an administrative and physical security system to prevent the unauthorized release of personal records.

The Privacy Act does apply to the records of every "individual," but—like FOIA—the Privacy Act only applies to records held by an "agency". Therefore, the records held by courts, executive components, Congress, or non-agency government entities are not subject to the provisions in the Privacy Act and there is no right to these records.

Chapter 9

ACCESS TO INFORMATION: LIST OF CASES

- Miami Student v. Miami University, 79 Ohio St. 3d 168, 680 N.E.2d 956 (OH Sup Ct 1997)
- United States v. Miami University, 294 F. 3d 797 (6th Cir. 2002)
- ESPN, Inc., v. Ohio State Univ., 132 Ohio St. 3d 212 (OH Sup Ct 2012)
- State ex rel. Schiffbauer v. Banaszak, 142 Ohio St. 3d 535; 2015-Ohio-1854; 33 N.E.3d 52; 2015 Ohio LEXIS 1332 (OH Sup Ct May 2015)
- Center for National Security Studies v. U.S. Dept. of Justice, 331 F. 3d 918 (U.S. App. 2003)
- National Archives & Records Administration v. Favish, 541 U.S. 157 (2004)

CASE LAW NOTES TEMPLATE

1. Description: What triggered the dispute? Who (full names and titles of plaintiffs; location; time frame) sued whom (full names and titles of defendants) and why (with specific examples/details)? What were the plaintiff/appellee/petitioner's arguments? What were defendant/appellant/respondent's arguments?

2. Resolution: Which court made the final decision; what the final court decision was (i.e., who won and why; specific reasons how the court reached its decision (the court's rationale))?

3. Significance: What effect this court decision has had on this particular First Amendment issue?

4. Application: How would you apply this court's rationale in this specific decision to future cases involving this same First Amendment issue (or to a hypothetical situation posed on your exam)?

CHAPTER 10

CONFIDENTIALITY

CONFIDENTIALITY: PROTECTING SOURCES; KEEPING PROMISES

"Freedom of the press is a hollow concept unless it includes freedom to gather the news. And that freedom, in turn, is hollow if prosecutors are permitted to turn reporters into government investigators by regularly hauling them before grand juries." —Wolfson, Andrew. "1972: Paul Branzburg's Secret," *Louisville (KY) Courier Journal,* September 17, 1987, pp. 1, 13

JARGON TERMS		
• Confidentiality • Grand jury v. petit jury	• Shield law • Subpoena v. search warrant • Contempt of court	• Concurring opinion • Dicta

Reporter's Privilege THREE-PART TEST **Branzburg v. Hayes (1972)**
1. Reporter has information relevant to hearing 2. Government has compelling need for information 3. Government cannot get information from any other source

"We discern a lurking and subtle threat to journalists and their employers if disclosure of outtakes, notes, and other unused information, even if non-confidential, becomes routine and casually . . . compelled."
—U.S. Supreme Court Justice Lewis Powell, Branzburg v. Hayes, 1972)

News War: Secrets, & Spin: Part One

PBS. Frontline
Air date: February 13, 2007
Segment 1: Confidentiality and *Branzburg v. Hayes* (1972)
Concepts to Consider; Concepts to Know:
• Role of confidentiality in news gathering
• Waivers for sources
• Earl Caldwell and the Black Panthers
• *Branzburg v. Hayes* (1972)
• Media used as an "arm of law enforcement"
• Justice Powell's dicta in *Branzburg*
• Reporter's privilege and state shield laws
• Guidelines before issuing a subpoena to force a journalist to testify

PRIVACY PROTECTION ACT OF 1980
• Requirement for federal, state and local police • Must get a subpoena • Cannot rely on just a simple search warrant
EXCEPTIONS: 1. Police believe reporter committed crime 2. Police believe material will be destroyed 3. Involves immediate danger

News War: Secrets, & Spin: Part One

PBS. Frontline
Air date: February 13, 2007
Segment 2: Plamegate
In re Special Counsel Investigation (Judith Miller) (2005)

Time

- Time Frame: 2003-2005
- Media coverage of weapons of mass destruction (WMD)
- January 28, 2003: Bush's—State of the Union Address
- 16-word sentence: "The British government has learned that Saddam Hussein recently sought significant quantities of uranium from Africa."
- Used as rationale for President Bush's decision to go to war in Iraq.
- Media sought to see if this statement was accurate

The Players

- Husband: Ex-diplomat and former ambassador Joe Wilson
- Wilson's wife: Secret CIA agent Valerie (Wilson) Plame
- Chicago Sun Times columnist: Robert D. Novak (identified wife as CIA agent)
- Judith Miller (*New York Times*)
- Matthew Palmer (*Time* magazine)
- Special Prosecutor Patrick J. Fitzgerald

The Dispute:

- Wilson wrote a NYT opinion piece saying WMD/Africa story false
- As "punishment": confidential sources in the White House leaked his wife's name as a CIA agent (secret identity) to the media (a crime)
- Justice Department opened an investigation
- Wanted to know who leaked CIA agent Valerie Plame's identity
- Subpoenaed various Miller and Palmer to find out
- Test of *Branzburg v. Hayes*
- First Amendment issue: Do reporters have First Amendment right to withhold information from investigators during **criminal** proceedings?

Possible Suspects

- Karl Rove, Deputy Chief of Staff, Office of President
- Lewis "Scooter" Libby, Chief of Staff, Office of Vice President
- Vice President Dick Cheney

OHIO SHIELD LAW (PRINT)
2739.12 Newspaper reporters not required to reveal source of information.

No person engaged in the work of, or connected with, or employed by any newspaper or any press association for the purpose of gathering, procuring, compiling, editing, disseminating, or publishing news shall be required to disclose the source of any information procured or obtained by such person in the course of his employment, in any legal proceeding, trial, or investigation before any court, grand jury, petit jury, or any officer thereof, before the presiding officer of any tribunal, or his agent, or before any commission, department, division, or bureau of this state, or before any county or municipal body, officer or committee thereof.

Effective Date: 10-01-1953

Legal citation: Newspaper reporters not required to reveal source of information, Ohio Rev. Code § 2739.12.

© Lawriter LLC. Reprinted by permission.

OHIO SHIELD LAW (BROADCAST)
2739.04 Disclosure of new source.

No person engaged in the work of, or connected with, or employed by any noncommercial educational or commercial radio broadcasting station, or any noncommercial educational or commercial television broadcasting station, or network of such stations, for the purpose of gathering, procuring, compiling, editing, disseminating, publishing, or broadcasting news shall be required to disclose the source of any information procured or obtained by such person in the course of his employment, in any legal proceeding, trial, or investigation before any court, grand jury, petit jury, or any officer thereof, before the presiding officer of any tribunal, or his agent, or before any commission, department, division, or bureau of this state, or before any county or municipal body, officer, or committee thereof.

Every noncommercial educational or commercial radio broadcasting station, and every noncommercial educational or commercial television broadcasting station shall maintain for a period of six months from the date of its broadcast thereof, a record of those statements of information the source of which was procured or obtained by persons employed by the station in gathering, procuring, compiling, editing, disseminating, publishing, or broadcasting news.

As used in this section:

A. "Record" includes a tape, disc, script, or any other item or document that sets forth the content of the statements that are required by this section to be recorded.

B. "Noncommercial educational television or radio broadcasting station" means a television or radio broadcast station that is licensed by the federal communications commission as a noncommercial educational radio or television broadcast station, transmits only noncommercial programs for educational purposes, and is owned and operated by:

   1. A public agency or institution or nonprofit private foundation, corporation, or association;

   2. A municipal corporation.

Effective Date: 11-11-1977

Legal citation: Disclosure of News Source, Ohio Rev. Code § 2739.04.

© Lawriter LLC. Reprinted by permission.

Chapter 10

CONFIDENTIALITY: LIST OF CASES

- Branzburg v. Hayes (In Re Pappas and U.S. v. Caldwell), 408 U.S. 665 (1972)
- U.S. v. Sterling, 724 F. 3d 482 (4th Cir 2013)
- Zurcher v. Stanford Daily, 98 S. Ct. 1970 (1978)
- Cohen v. Cowles Media, 111 S. Ct. 2513 (1991)

CASE LAW NOTES TEMPLATE

1. Description: What triggered the dispute? Who (full names and titles of plaintiffs; location; time frame) sued whom (full names and titles of defendants) and why (with specific examples/details)? What were the plaintiff/appellee/petitioner's arguments? What were defendant/appellant/respondent's arguments?

2. Resolution: Which court made the final decision; what the final court decision was (i.e., who won and why; specific reasons how the court reached its decision (the court's rationale))?

3. Significance: What effect this court decision has had on this particular First Amendment issue?

4. Application: How would you apply this court's rationale in this specific decision to future cases involving this same First Amendment issue (or to a hypothetical situation posed on your exam)?

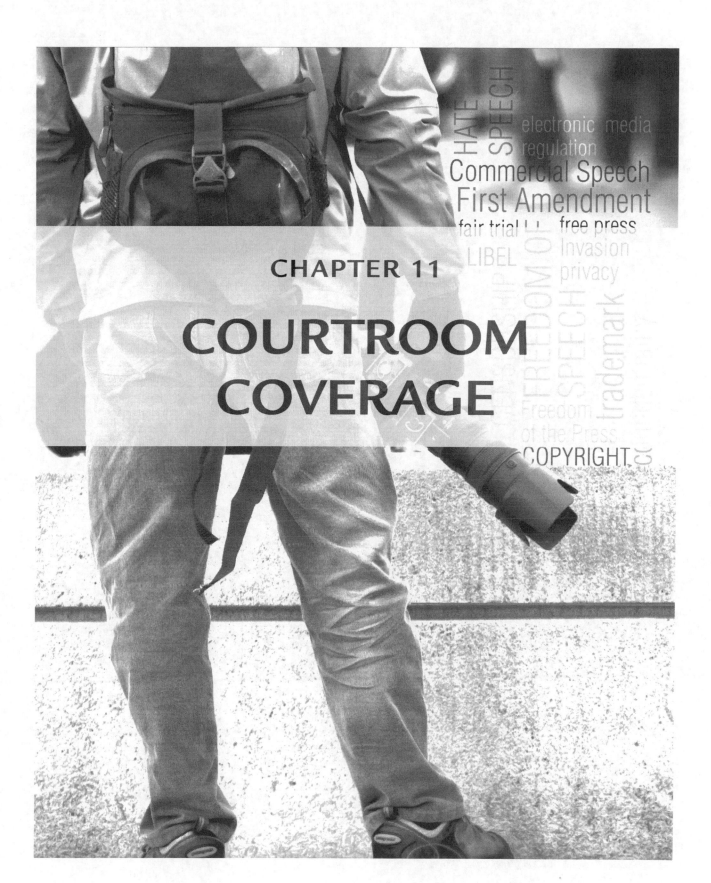

CHAPTER 11

COURTROOM COVERAGE

BALANCING FIRST AMENDMENT WITH SIXTH AMENDMENT

First Amendment		Sixth Amendment
"Congress shall make no law abridging . . . freedom of speech and of the press."	 Yulia Glam / Shutterstock.com	• Fair trial • Speedy trial • Public trial • Impartial Jury

AMENDMENT VI

In all criminal prosecutions, the accused shall enjoy the right to a speedy and public trial, by an impartial jury of the State and district wherein the crime shall have been committed; which district shall have been previously ascertained by law, and to be informed of the nature and cause of the accusation; to be confronted with the witnesses against him; to have compulsory process for obtaining witnesses in his favor, and to have the assistance of counsel for his defense.

DEFENDANT'S RIGHTS UNDER THE SIXTH AMENDMENT

- Speedy trial
- Public trial
- Impartial jury
- Trial held in the same state/district where crime was committed
- Formally charged
- Confronted with witnesses
- Defense attorney
- Defense witnesses

JUDICIAL REMEDIES TO PROTECT JURORS FROM IMPACT OF PREJUDICIAL PRETRIAL PUBLICITY

- Changing trial location (change of venue)
- Importing jury (change of venire)
- Delaying trial (continuance)
- Excusing potential jurors who demonstrate bias (*voir dire*)
- Admonishing jurors (jury instructions)
- Sequestering jurors
- Scheduling new trial
- Conducting different trials for defendants charged with same crime
- Holding violators of court order in contempt (fine and/or jail)

FOUR FACTORS JUDGE DECIDING WHETHER TO CLOSE COURTROOM

1. Courtroom proceedings presumed open. Closing the courtroom is only allowed when necessary to protect an overriding interest or higher value
2. Closure order must be narrowly tailored—no broader than necessary
3. Trial court must consider reasonable alternatives before closing the courtroom
4. Closure order must be supported by facts—not mere speculation that closure is required

Chapter 11

COURTROOM COVERAGE: LIST OF CASES

- Sheppard v. Maxwell, 384 U.S. 333 (1966)
- Nebraska Press v. Stuart, 427 U.S. 53 (1976)
- Richmond Newspapers v. Virginia, 448 U.S. 555 (1980)

CASE LAW NOTES TEMPLATE

1. Description: What triggered the dispute? Who (full names and titles of plaintiffs; location; time frame) sued whom (full names and titles of defendants) and why (with specific examples/details). What were the plaintiff/appellee/petitioner's arguments? What were defendant/appellant/respondent's arguments?

2. Resolution: Which court made the final decision; what the final court decision was (i.e., who won and why; specific reasons how the court reached its decision (the court's rationale))?

3. Significance: What effect this court decision has had on this particular First Amendment issue?

4. Application: How would you apply this court's rationale in this specific decision to future cases involving this same First Amendment issue (or to a hypothetical situation posed on your exam)?

CHAPTER 12

COMMERCIAL SPEECH

COMMERCIAL SPEECH: ADVERTISING REGULATION

COMMERCIAL SPEECH

- Advertising of products or services
- Hardier than political speech; can withstand government regulation
- "Less central to interests of First Amendment"

"Speech does not lose its First Amendment protection because money is spent to project it, as in a paid advertisement of one form or another."
—Virginia State Board of Pharmacy v. Virginia Citizens Consumer Council, 1976

COMMERCIAL SPEECH DOCTRINE

Government may regulate:
- Advertising that is false or misleading
- Ads for unlawful goods or services
- Some TRUTHFUL advertising
- False Advertising: no First Amendment protection
- Remember Meiklejohnian theory

Rank Order of First Amendment Protection

MOST PROTECTION:	• **Political speech** • Ideas; opinions; Hate speech; Symbolic speech • Print media; Internet
SOME PROTECTION	• Cable
LESS PROTECTION:	• **Commercial speech** • Pornography • Broadcast media
<u>EVEN LESS</u> PROTECTION	• **Advertising for legal—but harmful--products (i.e., tobacco, gambling, alcohol)**
<u>NO</u> PROTECTION:	• **False advertising; false facts about individuals, products, or businesses** • Fighting words; hate crimes • Obscenity; child pornography

CENTRAL HUDSON TEST

Central Hudson Gas & Electric Co. v. Public Service Commission of New York, 100 S. Ct. 2343 (1980)

1. Is ad false or advertise illegal products (e.g., cocaine, murder)?
2. Does government have good reasons to ban the ad?
3. Is regulation working? Is it solving the problem?
4. Does regulation control the problem without violating the free speech rights of others?

FEDERAL TRADE COMMISSION

- Promotes fair competition; Prevents deceptive business practices; Regulates packaging and labeling
- **<u>Regulates false/deceptive advertising</u>**

Bratovanov / Shutterstock.com

DECEPTIVE ADVERTISING

"Presenting a test, experiment or demonstration that . . . is represented to the public as actual proof of a claim made for a product which is material to inducing sale and is not in fact a genuine test, experiment or demonstration being conducted as represented."

—FTC v. Colgate Palmolive (1965)/"Rapid Shave" case

WHO CAN BE SUED FOR DECEPTIVE (FALSE) ADVERTISING?

• Competitors; Advertising companies; Celebrities in testimonials

Chapter 12

COMMERCIAL SPEECH: LIST OF CASES

- Central Hudson Gas & Electric Co. v. Public Service Commission of New York, 100 S. Ct. 2343 (1980)
- Braun v. Soldier of Fortune Magazine, 968 F.2d 1110 (U.S. App. 11th Cir 1992)
- Telebrands Corp. v. FTC, 457 F.3d 354; 2006 U.S. App. LEXIS 20136 (4th Cir 2006)
- POM Wonderful v. Coca-Cola, Co., 134 S. Ct. 2228 (2014)

CASE LAW NOTES TEMPLATE

1. Description: What triggered the dispute? Who (full names and titles of plaintiffs; location; time frame) sued whom (full names and titles of defendants) and why (with specific examples/details)? What were the plaintiff/appellee/petitioner's arguments? What were defendant/appellant/respondent's arguments?

2. Resolution: Which court made the final decision; what the final court decision was (i.e., who won and why; specific reasons how the court reached its decision (the court's rationale))?

3. Significance: What effect this court decision has had on this particular First Amendment issue?

4. Application: How would you apply this court's rationale in this specific decision to future cases involving this same First Amendment issue (or to a hypothetical situation posed on your exam)?

Chapter 12

TOBACCO ADVERTISING: LIST OF CASES

- Posadas de Puerto Rico Associates v. Tourism Co. of Puerto Rico, 447 U.S. 557 (1980)
- Janet C. Mangini v. R. J. Reynolds Tobacco Company, 875 P.2d 73; 1994 Cal. LEXIS 3160 (1994)
- Lorillard Tobacco Co. v. Reilly, 533 U.S. 525; 121 S. Ct. 2404; 150 L. Ed. 2d 532; (2001)
- R.J. Reynolds Tobacco Co. v. FDA, 696 F.3d 1205; 2012 U.S. App. LEXIS 17925 (U.S. App. D.C. 2012)
- U.S. v. Philip Morris USA, 449 F. Supp. 2d 1, 909 (D.D.C. 2009) ("Injunction Opinion")

CASE LAW NOTES TEMPLATE

1. Description: What triggered the dispute? Who (full names and titles of plaintiffs; location; time frame) sued whom (full names and titles of defendants) and why (with specific examples/details)? What were the plaintiff/appellee/petitioner's arguments? What were defendant/appellant/respondent's arguments?

2. Resolution: Which court made the final decision; what the final court decision was (i.e., who won and why; specific reasons how the court reached its decision (the court's rationale))?

3. Significance: What effect this court decision has had on this particular First Amendment issue?

4. Application: How would you apply this court's rationale in this specific decision to future cases involving this same First Amendment issue (or to a hypothetical situation posed on your exam)?

RetroClipArt / Shutterstock.com

CHAPTER 13

INTELLECTUAL PROPERTY

COPYRIGHT

"[t]o promote the Progress of Science and useful Arts, by securing for limited Times to Authors and Inventors the exclusive Right to their respective Writings and Discoveries"

—U.S. Constitution, art. I, § 8, cl. 8.

- Copyright protection is automatic under U.S. law and international treaties
- Advisable to include a copyright notice in prominent place of work
- Author's life plus 70 years (as of 1998)
- Need permission to use; Pay royalties to author
- Public domain: Material no longer under copyright and can be used without paying royalties; freely available for public use

WHAT CAN BE COPYRIGHTED

- Derivative works
- Compilations (i.e., databases, trivia dictionaries)
- Collective works
- Prose (fiction and non-fiction); Poetry
- Sound recordings; musical works/lyrics; pantomimes; choreographic works
- Plays; scripts; photography; graphics; paintings; sculptures
- Radio/television productions; newspaper/magazine articles (descriptions of news events)
- Advertising layouts; Computer software
- Motion pictures; videos; maps: architectural designs

WHAT CANNOT BE COPYRIGHTED

- News
- Factual
- Historical information
- Ideas
- Trademarks/service marks (falls under trademark law)

Sonny Bono Copyright Term Extension Act (CTEA) 1998

- Retroactively extended term of copyright by 20 years
- Author's life plus 70 years (formerly 50 years)
- Eldred v. Ashcroft (2001): Court challenge to CTEA
  Opponents say CTEA is unconstitutional because:
- Retroactively extending copyright to works that should already have fallen into the public domain restricts speech
- Copyright extension is too long and, as a result, restricts speech
  Supporters say it is important to continue to protect priceless works:
- Novels such as *The Great Gatsby*
- Movies such as *The Jazz Singer*
- Cartoon characters such as Mickey Mouse and Pluto

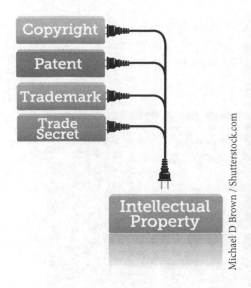

Michael D Brown / Shutterstock.com

s_bukley / Shutterstock.com

Chapter 13

COPYRIGHT & FAIR USE: LIST OF CASES

- Eldred v. Ashcroft, 123 S. Ct. 769 (2003)
- A&M Records, Inc. v. Napster, 284 F. 3d 1091 (U.S. App. 9th Cir. 2002)
- Metro-Goldwyn-Mayer Studios Inc., v. Grokster, Ltd., 2005 U.S. LEXIS 5212 (2005)
- Campbell v. Acuff-Rose Music Co., 114 S. Ct. 1164 (1994)
- Video-Cinema Films v. CNN, 2001 U.S. Dist. LEXIS 15937 (SDNY 2001)
- Pharrell Williams, et al. v. Bridgeport Music, Inc., et al. 2015 U.S. Dist LEXIS 97262 (Dist Ct CA, 2015)
- Lenz v. Universal Music Corp. , 2015 U.S. Dis LEXIS 97262 (Dist Ct CA, 2015)

CASE LAW NOTES TEMPLATE

1. Description: What triggered the dispute? Who (full names and titles of plaintiffs; location; time frame) sued whom (full names and titles of defendants) and why (with specific examples/details)? What were the plaintiff/appellee/petitioner's arguments? What were defendant/appellant/respondent's arguments?

2. Resolution: Which court made the final decision; what the final court decision was (i.e., who won and why; specific reasons how the court reached its decision (the court's rationale))?

3. Significance: What effect this court decision has had on this particular First Amendment issue?

4. Application: How would you apply this court's rationale in this specific decision to future cases involving this same First Amendment issue (or to a hypothetical situation posed on your exam)?

Jason Winter / Shutterstock.com

168stock / Shutterstock.com

PlusONE / Shutterstock.com

Chapter 13

TRADEMARK: LIST OF CASES

- Kellogg Co. v. Exxon Corp., 209 F.3d 562 (6th Cir 1999)
- ETW Corp. v. Jireh Publishing, Inc., 332 F.3d 915 (6th Cir 2003)
- Fox News Network v. Penguin Group, Inc., 2003 U.S. Dist. LEXIS 18693 (S.D. NY 2003)

CASE LAW NOTES TEMPLATE

1. Description: What triggered the dispute? Who (full names and titles of plaintiffs; location; time frame) sued whom (full names and titles of defendants) and why (with specific examples/details). What were the plaintiff/appellee/petitioner's arguments? What were defendant/appellant/respondent's arguments?

2. Resolution: Which court made the final decision; what the final court decision was (i.e., who won and why; specific reasons how the court reached its decision (the court's rationale))?

3. Significance: What effect this court decision has had on this particular First Amendment issue?

4. Application: How would you apply this court's rationale in this specific decision to future cases involving this same First Amendment issue (or to a hypothetical situation posed on your exam)?

Michael D Brown / Shutterstock.com

CHAPTER 14

OBSCENITY, PORNOGRAPHY & VIOLENCE

Chapter 14

OBSCENITY, PORNGRAPHY & VIOLENCE: LIST OF CASES

- Miller v. California, 413 U.S. 15 (1973)
- Hudnut v. American Booksellers, 475 U.S. 1001 (1986)
- U.S. v. Playboy, 529 U.S. 803,120 S. Ct. 1878, 146 L. Ed. 2d 865 (2000)
- Ashcroft v. Free Speech Coalition, 122 S. Ct. 1389 (2002)
- U.S. v. Stevens, 130 S. Ct. 1577, 176 L. Ed. 2d 435 (2010)

CASE LAW NOTES TEMPLATE

1. Description: What triggered the dispute? Who (full names and titles of plaintiffs; location; time frame) sued whom (full names and titles of defendants) and why (with specific examples/details)? What were the plaintiff/appellee/petitioner's arguments? What were defendant/appellant/respondent's arguments?

2. Resolution: Which court made the final decision; what the final court decision was (i.e., who won and why; specific reasons how the court reached its decision (the court's rationale))?

3. Significance: What effect this court decision has had on this particular First Amendment issue?

4. Application: How would you apply this court's rationale in this specific decision to future cases involving this same First Amendment issue (or to a hypothetical situation posed on your exam)?

squarelogo / Shutterstock.com

CHAPTER 15

LEGAL RESEARCH

UNDERSTANDING THE LEGAL CITATION

Yulia Glam / Shutterstock.com

Common (or Case) Law

Common law or **case** law is created by the judicial branch of government—federal courts, state courts, local courts. To find court cases quickly it's important to remember how:

- a lawsuit makes its way through the judicial system
- how to read a **legal citation**

THE LEGAL CITATION

- Court cases are cataloged differently from other types of sources like books and magazines
- Each individual court decision has it's own special identifier—sort of like a call number or social security number—called a **legal citation**
- The **legal citation** is a uniform system used by the judicial branch to cite each court decision from the trial court to the U.S. Supreme Court; whether it's a federal court case or state court case.
- Understanding the legal citation can help you develop more precise search strategies
- Knowing a specific court decision makes finding the full text to that decision "super simple"—especially if you are using the legal citation as your search term in the appropriate electronic reference source.
- For example, let's examine each part of the following legal citation:

CURTIS PUBLISHING COMPANY, Petitioner v. WALLACE BUTTS, Respondent, 388 US 130,18 L.Ed.2d 1094, 84 S.Ct. 1975 (1967)		
Curtis Publishing Company	Plaintiff (Trial Level) Appellant (Appeals Level) Petitioner (Sup. Ct. Level)	The person who initiated the legal action
Wallace Butts	Defendant (Trial Level) Appellee (Appeals Level) Respondent (Sup. Ct. Level)	The individual "being sued" or who is having to defend himself/herself at the appeals level
SPECIAL NOTES: • There can be more than one **plaintiff** and **defendant,** but usually only the last name of the first person in each party will be given in the citation. • For trial court decisions, the first name listed is the plaintiff. But when cases are appealed, the names can reverse order (or change altogether) depending on who asked the appellate court to hear the case.		

US	Abbreviation of the book (called a court reporter) where the full text of this court decision can be found. The "US" in this legal citation is the abbreviation for a court reporter entitled *United States Reports*.
388	Volume number of the court reporter entitled *United States Reports* where the full text of this court decision can be found
130	Page number of volume 388 of *United States Reports* where the full text this court decision can be found

So if you were to go a law library (or another library that had *United States Reports* in its collection) you would:

- Locate *United States Reports* in the library's stacks
- Take volume 388 off the shelf
- Turn to page 130

There you would find the **full text** of the U.S. Supreme Court's decision in *Curtis v. Butts*.

18 L.Ed.2d 1094	Parallel citation to the full text of this same case. If you looked in volume 18 of the court reporter entitled *United States Supreme Court Reports Lawyers Edition 2ⁿᵈ Series* and turned to page 1094, you would find the full text of this <u>exact</u> court decision.
84 S.Ct. 1975	Another parallel citation to the full text of this same case. If you took volume 84 of a court reporter entitled *Supreme Court Reporter* and turned to page 1975, you would find the full text of this <u>exact</u> court decision.

Parallel citations come in handy if you don't have access to an electronic legal reference source and you have to find the court decision using the "old-fashioned" print version. If your library doesn't have *Supreme Court Reporter* in its collection but does have *United States Supreme Court ReportsLawyers Edition 2ⁿᵈ Series,* you can still find the full text to this same court decision using the L. Ed. 2d parallel citation. For example, Alden Library on the OU Athens campus only has *Supreme Court Reporter* in its collection—but not *United States Supreme Court Reports Lawyers Edition 2ⁿᵈ Series* or *United States Reports*.

(1967)	**The year this court decision was decided**

You can learn a lot from a legal citation. If the abbreviation of the Court Reporter is		
F. Supp.	The case was decided at the	<u>Federal</u> district (trial) level
F. 2d; F. 3d	The case was decided at the	<u>Federal</u> appeals Court level
Ohio Appeals	The case was decided at the	Ohio State appeals court level
Oh. St.	The case was decided at the	Ohio State Supreme Court level
U.S.; L. Ed. 2d; S. Ct.	The case was decided at the	U.S. Supreme Court level

HOW TO WRITE A PROPER LEGAL CITATION FOR CASE/COMMON LAW

When you findthe full-text of a state or federal law, the first page will look something like this:

John J. Scaccia, et al., Plaintiffs-Appellants v. Dayton Newspaper, Inc., et al., Defendants-Appellees
C.A. Case Nos. 18435 & 18729
Court of Appeals of Ohio, Second Appellate District, Montgomery County
2001 Ohio 1834; 30 Media L.Rep. 1172
November 30, 2001, Rendered

You have all the information you need to write a legal citation to this court decision in its proper format. In fact you have **MORE** than what you need to write this legal citation in its proper format. The complete legal citation that you could use for this court case would look like this:

John J. Scaccia v. Dayton Newspaper, Inc., 30 Media L. Rep. 1172 (2001).

Notice that I used only one of the two legal citations. Either one would be correct, or I could have included both of them. Either citation would give you the full text to this particular lawsuit.

TIPS FOR USING PRINT LEGAL SOURCES

You never can tell when your computer will crash or the Internet connection will "freeze." You should **never** be so dependent on the Internet that you are unable to find quality legal sources the "good old fashioned" way. Should you not have access to the Internet, your "plan B" would be to find your court case using the appropriate **print** legal reference sources.

In order to use the print version of legal reference sources efficiently you need to know:

- **where the closest law library or university or public library (that has legal documents in its collection) is located**
- **which legal reference source to use**
- **how the print reference source is organized**
- **how to use the print reference source**
- **how to find the full text of the government document you need**

NOTE: The Athens County Law Library is located on the top floor of the Athens County Courthouse on Court St.

Know **which** legal reference source to use

- **For common law/case law**	- Various state court reporters - National Reporter System (see complete listing at end of this section)

PRINT REFERENCE SOURCES FOR FINDING FEDERAL CASE LAW

United States Supreme Court decisions	- *United States Reports* (U.S.) - *United States Supreme Court Reports, Lawyers'* (L.Ed.,L.Ed. 2d) - *Supreme Court Reporter* (S.Ct.) - *United States Law Week* (U.S.L.W.)

United States appeals courts decisions	• *Federal Reporter* (F., F. 2d., F. 3d)
United States district courts decisions	• *Federal Supplement* (F. Supp.)

PRINT REFERENCE SOURCES FOR FINDING STATE CASE LAW

Atlantic Reporter (A.)	• Conn., Del., Me., Md., N.H., N.J., Pa., R.I., Vt., D.C.
California Reporter (Cal. Rptr.)	• Calif. Sup. Ct., Courts of Appeal and Appellate Dept. of the Superior Court
New York Supplement (N.Y. Supp.)	• N.Y. (all state courts). Since 1932, the N.Y. Court of Appeals opinions are published here as well as in the *North Eastern* Reporter
North Eastern Reporter *(N.E., N.E. 2d)*	• Ill., Ind., Mass., N.Y., and Ohio
North Western Reporter *(N.W.)*	• Iowa, Mich., Minn., Neb., N.D., S.D., Wis.
Pacific Reporter (P., P.2d)	• Alaska, Ariz., Cal. to 1960, Calif. Sup. Ct. since 1960, Colo., Hawaii, Idaho, Kan., Mont., Nev., N.M., Okla., Or., Utah, Wash., Wyo.
South Eastern Reporter (S.E.)	• Ga., N.C., S.C., Va., W.Va.
South Western Reporter (S.W.)	• Ark., Ky., Mo., Tenn., Tex.
Southern Reporter (So.)	• Ala., Fla., La., Miss.

The Federal Circuit Court System

- Eleven circuits, divided geographically
- One District of Columbia circuit
- One federal circuit [hears only specific types of cases and appeals from district courts in cases where the federal government is being sued (the defendant)]

First Circuit: Maine, Massachusetts, New Hampshire, Puerto Rico, Rhode Island

Second Circuit: Connecticut, New York, Vermont

Third Circuit: Delaware, New Jersey, Pennsylvania, Virgin Islands

Fourth Circuit: Maryland, North Carolina, South Carolina, West Virginia, Virginia

Fifth Circuit: Louisiana, Mississippi, Texas

Sixth Circuit: **Kentucky, Michigan, Ohio, Tennessee**

Seventh Circuit: Illinois, Indiana, Wisconsin

Eighth Circuit: Arkansas, Iowa, Minnesota, Missouri, Nebraska, North Dakota, South Dakota

Ninth Circuit: Alaska, Arizona, California, Guam, Hawaii, Idaho, Montana, Nevada, Northern Mariana Islands, Oregon, Washington

Tenth Circuit: Colorado, Kansas, New Mexico, Oklahoma, Utah, Wyoming

Eleventh Circuit: Alabama, Florida, Georgia

CHAPTER 16

THE ANALYSIS PAPER

GENERAL INSTRUCTIONS
- Analysis Paper assignment is posted on your **J3100/5100 Blackboard** site.
- Submit your paper as an e-mail (Microsoft Word) attachment to <u>dashiell@ohio.edu</u>.
- <u>**PLEASE put your name, e-mail address, and page number in header of your paper.**</u>
- **SAVE** your e-mail with the date/time stamp just in case you need to re-submit your paper and verify that you submitted your paper by the established deadline.
- Refer to your syllabus for policies on deadlines and plagiarism.
- Assignment instructions, deadline and grading criteria are also posted under your *Blackboard* **"Contents"** link→**"Analysis Paper"** folder.
- Refer to your **Bl***ackboard* **"Contents"** link→**"Analysis Paper"** folder for additional hints and FAQs for researching and writing your analysis paper.

RESEARCH HINTS
- **CAUTION!!** This assignment is <u>**not**</u> designed to be completed the night (or week) before it is due; you need to start researching for this paper early (i.e., the day it is discussed in class).
- Choose your search terms carefully. A focused Boolean search strategy will give you stronger results with fewer research headaches. The goal is to find the most relevant case law possible as efficiently as possible (without wasting a lot of time).
- Make sure that your selected court cases are relevant for this narrow paper topic.
- For some reason Lexis-Nexis likes the keyword "defamation" better than the keyword "libel."
- Carefully read and refer to all the other handouts (i.e., FAQs, legal citations, etc.) posted on **Blackboard** for this assignment.

FINDING RELEVANT CASE LAW USING LEXIS-NEXIS ACADEMIC

One way to find <u>appropriate and relevant libel</u> court cases:
- Go to **Lexis-Nexis Academic** (on the Ohio University Libraries web page)
- In left-hand column (blue with white lettering), click: **US Legal**
- Select: **Federal & State Cases**
- Under **Search For**: enter your search terms with the appropriate Boolean connectors (i.e., and, or, not), within same paragraph).
- Under **Specify Date**: You may limit by date (optional)
- Under **Jurisdiction**, select: **6th Circuit <u>or</u> one of the states in the 6th Circuit**
- From the list of case citations select <u>**relevant**</u> court cases in which the defendant (i.e., journalist, news organization, or a non-media individual/business) is being sued <u>and</u> the court has to actually decide on whether the plaintiff is public or private figure. This court decision must also provide <u>details and a thorough explanation</u> of the court's rationale explaining why the plaintiff (i.e., attorney or school employee should be (or should not be) treated as a public official or a public figure for the purpose of the libel suit.

GRADING CRITERIA FOR DR. D'S. LEGAL ANALYSIS PAPERS (100 pts.)

A: (90–100)	<ul><li>Strong focus; excellent writing style; excellent translation of complicated legal jargon</li><li>Demonstrates excellent understanding of the material</li><li>Demonstrates excellent independent thought and personal analysis</li><li>Demonstrates ability to conduct thorough, quality legal research, relying on <u>primary sources</u> (i.e., the actual court decisions, government documents) rather than secondary sources (i.e., the text book, newspaper articles, class lecture notes and handouts)</li><li>Selected court cases relevant to the topic, correctly interpreted and discussed, and cited in proper legal citation format <u>as discussed in class</u></li><li>No excessive "copying and pasting" of material; no evidence of plagiarism</li><li>Turned in by established deadline</li></ul>
B: (79–89)	<ul><li>Acceptable but not sophisticated word choice</li><li>Acceptable use of primary sources</li><li>Stresses more summary than personal analysis</li><li>Contains some repetitious, rambling, and/or irrelevant content</li><li>Contains above-average use of intelligence and creativity</li><li>Demonstrates good understanding of material and ability to apply relevant legal concepts to research topic</li><li>Selected court cases relevant to topic; correctly interpreted and discussed; and cited in proper legal citation format <u>as discussed in class/assignment handouts</u></li><li>No excessive "copying and pasting" of material; no evidence of plagiarism</li><li>Missed deadline</li></ul>
C: (69–78)	<ul><li>Poor focus; "skimpy" analysis; not enough detail</li><li>Relied too much on textbook/secondary sources instead of primary sources</li><li>Legal position supported with only assertions—without evidence, sourcing or adequate analysis</li><li>Just transcribed another author's work with little evidence of personal analysis, evidence or sourcing</li><li>Contains too much repetitious, rambling, and/or irrelevant content</li><li>Excessive "copying/pasting" of articles (in whole or in part) from the Internet with no evidence of re-writing or personal analysis</li><li>Excessive use of long direct quotes with little paraphrasing or personal analysis. Too much reliance on other authors' interpretations and words rather than using your own paraphrasing to convince instructor that you understand the content.</li><li>Demonstrates fair understanding of material or ability to apply relevant legal concepts to research topic</li><li>Case law cited irrelevant or incorrectly interpreted</li></ul>

	• Case law not cited in proper legal citation format <u>as discussed in class/assignment handouts</u> • Missed deadline
D/F: (0–68)	• Little or significant evidence of preparation/research • No strong evidence of independent thought and personal analysis • Demonstrates weak understanding of the material with no ability to apply the relevant legal concepts to the research topic • No evidence of ability to conduct quality legal research • Excessive "copying/pasting" of articles (in whole or in part) from the Internet with no evidence of re-writing or personal analysis • Excessive use of long direct quotes with little paraphrasing or personal analysis. Too much reliance on other authors' interpretations and words rather than using your own paraphrasing to convince instructor that you understand the content. • Evidence of plagiarism in whole or in part • Numerous fact errors/misleading or confusing statements • Case law cited irrelevant or incorrectly interpreted • Case law not cited in proper legal citation format <u>as discussed in class</u> • Did not follow directions or meet assignment requirements • Missed deadline or not turned in at all

DR. D.'S GUIDE TO WRITING A <u>QUALITY</u> RESEARCH PAPER (updated: 3/2/12)

RESEARCH AND CONTENT

- Is **more** than just using your textbook, your class lecture notes, and/or a couple of books as sources (all secondary sources)
- Is **more** than using the first 2–5 newspaper or magazine articles you find
- **Uses more <u>primary</u> sources than secondary sources (i.e., researching the actual court decisions)**
- **Stays focused on the research question**
- Uses thorough research skills
- Should do more than simply "re-hash" what we have discussed in class
- Should do more than simply summarize or transcribe another author's work
- Should contain a thorough discussion and analysis of a topic that we were not able to discuss in great detail during class
- Should stay focused on the topic without taking too many "rabbit trails"

FORMAT

- All papers must be typed in 10–12 pt type
- Line spacing can be either single or double spaced (no preference)
- Length will vary depending on the topic and the course in which the paper is assigned. Focus on the content (i.e., thoroughly answering the question—not on how long the paper should be).

GENERAL RESEARCH HINTS:
- REMEMBER: Writing a short paper does **not** mean writing a "skimpy" paper.
- Start your research **early.** This is **not** a project you can do the night before it is due if you hope to do well.
- Rely on **primary sources**. Do not simply rely on another person's interpretation of a court case (i.e., case summaries on the Internet). One objective of this course is for you to demonstrate that you know how to conduct quality legal research (i.e., finding the actual court decisions, statutory or administrative laws; demonstrating that you understand court's rationale in making its decision; being able to translate the complex legal jargon into conversational (but sophisticated) language for the non-legal expert (i.e., a reporter or other media professional).
- Read each court decision **carefully** to make sure you understand the court's decision and rationale.
- When typing your paper on your computer, **save often** and keep a **backup** copy of your paper. If you are going to have computer problems, these problems will occur the night before your paper is due.
- Refer to your syllabus for policies on deadlines and plagiarism.
- Refer to separate handout for grading criteria.

CITING YOUR SOURCES

- Citations (footnotes, endnotes, or parenthetical references) within the paper are required.
- A list of "Works Cited" (bibliography) at the end of the paper or assignment is also required.
- Citations help the reader locate sources of material and lend authority/credibility to paper or presentation.
- Citations distinguish your ideas from others and prevent you from being charged with plagiarism.
- Cite **all** information that is not your "original" work (i.e., direct quotes, partial quotes, paraphrased information obtained from the source).
- You **must** cite your sources **throughout** the text of your paper as well as in your "works cited"/ bibliography.
- List citations for all sources you researched for your paper (including the court cases you discussed) in your "works cited"/bibliography.

What's a citation?

- A citation is a brief description of an information source, giving enough data to enable someone else to quickly and easily find the source. Here are some examples of typical kinds of data needed for different kinds of information sources:

Periodical Article	Book	Web Page
Article author(s)	Author(s)	Author(s)
Article title	Title	Date of publication
Periodical title	Edition (if given)	Title
Volume and issue number of periodical	Place of publication	URL
	Publisher	Date accessed
Date of issue	Date	
Pages		

Citations also have a specific format or style. **You will need to use a consistent citation style for your analysis paper.** The Ohio University Libraries web site is one source for finding citation style guides.

Every source—whether it's a book, a magazine article, an interview, a search engine, a video, a poster, or an electronic reference source—has an author and/or publisher and other bibliographical information necessary for a complete and proper citation.Guides to the various types of style will give you some guidance on how to cite these sources, but there will inevitably be types of sources they don't cover.

Remember, though, that the basic goal is to provide enough information to enable someone else to quickly and easily find the same source you used. The ability for someone else (i.e., your JOUR 3100/5100 instructor) to duplicate your research adds creditability to your paper.

BASIC LEGAL CITATION FORMS	
Cases:	**General Form**: the names of the parties (only the first plaintiff and defendant listed); the volume of the reporter, the abbreviation of the reporter; the page on which the case begins, the court, the year of the decision. Use parallel cites if the report is in more than one place or you are using an official report.
Sample Court Case Citations (judicial law):	Herbert v. Lando, 441 U.S. 153, 99 S.Ct. 1635 (1979) Salinger v. Random House, 811 F.2d 90 (2d Cir. 1987) Smith v. Jones, 727 F. Supp. 1407 (M.D. Tenn. 1987) Rancho LaCosta Inc. v. Superior Court, 6 Media L. Rep. 1351, 65 Cal. Rptr. 347 (1980) Newell v. Field Enterprises, 415 N.E.2d 434 (Ill. 1980)
Constitutions:	U.S. Const. Art II, Section 4 U.S. Const. Amend. I.
Codes (legislative law):	**General Form**: The name of the act (if you can find one); the volume, the specific code number, the section number, the year of publication of that volume of the code.
	Administrative Procedure Act, 22 U.S.C. § 2347 (1988) The Personal Rights Protection Act of 1984, Tenn. Code. Ann. § 47-25-1103(a) F.T.C. Federal Practices Act, 16 C.F.R. § 444 (1994) <unenacted bill example> H.R. 3055, 94th Congress, 2d Sess. § 3 (1976)
Books:	**General Form**: The names of the author(s); the title of the book; the city/state of publication; the publisher; the year of publication; any specific page references.
	W. Wat Hopkins (ed.) Communication and the Law. Northport, AL: Vision Press, 1998.
Periodicals (e.g., magazine or newspaper articles):	**General Form:** The names of the author(s), the title of the article, the name of the publication, the month and year of publication, page where the article begins and page of any quotation.
	John P. Stevens, The Freedom of Speech, 102 Yale L.J. 1293, 1297 (1993) Lynn Hirschberg, "The Misfit", Vanity Fair, Apr. 1991, at 158 Andrew Rosehthal, White House Tutors Kremlin in How a Presidency Works," New York Times, June 15, 1990, at Al, A7

NOTE: Finding the section symbol "§"	**For MS Word fonts on PCS:** • Hold down the "Alt" key and typing "0167" on the number keypad.
	• If that doesn't work, open the accessories menu in Windows, click on the key maps icon, select the font you are using, click on the character you want, and the keystroke will be displayed in the lower right corner of the window. **For MAC users:** • Hold down the "Alt/option" key and type the number 6 above the regular keypad. • If that doesn't work, go to the Apple menu; open the key caps file, then hold down the "Alt/option" key to show the special characters that can be accessed in that font.

USING WEB/INTERNET SOURCES

- **Not all web sites are good sources for a research paper.** Many are too simplistic for a research paper. Nothing more than summaries of summaries.
- Only select **credible** full-text web sites (i.e., **LEXIS-NEXIS Academic**)

CITING INTERNET SOURCES

- Cite all material that you find on the Internet in the same way you would cite any other article (i.e., author's name, title, date, page number, etc.)

- Do NOT cite the entire web site (i.e. Lexis-Nexis Academic, www.gigalaw.com). That would be the same thing as citing "Alden Library" as your source when you are citing a single book you checked out from Alden Library.

- Include the URL address in brackets at the end of your citation in your bibliography. Example: Dashiell, Eddith A. "How to Write a Media Law Paper," Dashiell Fantasy Times, Feb. 10, 2000, p. 26 [http://web.lexis-nexis.com/universe/, accessed November 22, 2010.]

- When citing page numbers from articles using the Internet, cite the specific page of the original (print version) of the document (if available). For example, if it is a newspaper/magazine article, cite the page numbers given for where the article appeared in the PRINTED version. If no page number is available, then don't include it.

- If you print an article from your computer, do not go by the page numbers at the bottom of the page (i.e., page 6 of 27). Those page numbers will not be consistent. If I printed the same case, my computer/printer may format the pages differently.